HOW DO WE KNOW
DINOSAURS EXISTED?

MIKE BENTON

SIMON & SCHUSTER
YOUNG BOOKS

First Published in 1993 by
Simon & Schuster Young Books

© 1993 Simon & Schuster Young Books
Simon & Schuster Young Books
Campus 400
Maylands Avenue
Hemel Hempstead
Hertfordshire
HP2 7EZ

A CIP catalogue record for this book is available from
the British Library

ISBN 0 7500 1300 1

Commissioning Editor: Thomas Keegan
Designer: Neville Graham
Editor: Kate Scarborough
Illustrators: John Butler and Alan Male

Typeset by Goodfellow & Egan, Cambridge
Printed and bound in Hong Kong

The words in *italic* are explained in the glossary
(apart from the Dinosaur names).

Contents

HOW DO WE KNOW
All about Dinosaurs?

DINOSAURS WERE BIG and they lived a long time ago. There were at least twenty different kinds of dinosaurs, and they were fierce brainless animals. They died out because they were hopeless failures.

These are the kinds of ideas that many people have about dinosaurs, and yet they are mainly wrong. Many dinosaurs were indeed big, but there were also small ones. Dinosaurs were in fact one of the most successful groups of animals of all time: they ruled the Earth for over 150 million years. They did indeed live a long time ago – long before the first humans.

And there were many different species of dinosaurs. Since the first discoveries of dinosaurs, palaeontologists (the scientists who study fossils) have named about 1000 species of dinosaurs from all continents on the Earth. Every year, another ten species are discovered.

Brachiosaurus
The largest well-known dinosaur, *Brachiosaurus* has been found in Tanzania (Africa) and in North America. It reached a length of 22.5 metres, and stood as tall as a three-storey building. A giant plant-eater.

Plateosaurus
One of the first large dinosaurs, *Plateosaurus* from Germany was a plant-eater. Some specimens were up to 8 metres long, but many were smaller. *Plateosaurus* used its strong hands to gather leaves from tall trees.

Compsognathus
A small rare dinosaur from Germany and France, known from only a couple of specimens. *Compsognathus*, at 1.4 metres long, is one of the smallest dinosaurs.

Stegosaurus
One of the most famous plant-eating dinosaurs from North America. *Stegosaurus* was up to 7.5 metres long, and had a double row of bone plates down the middle of its back. These may have been for defence, or for temperature control.

Triceratops
A large, 9-metre long plant-eater from North America. Its long horns may have been used in fighting, and the heavy bony plate at the back of the skull may have helped protect the neck.

Pteranodon
Not a dinosaur, but a pterosaur, or flying reptile. It came from North America and had a wingspan of 7 metres, larger than any bird and more like a hang-glider.

DINOSAUR CLASSIFICATION
All dinosaurs are related to each other. They arose from a single *ancestor* about 230 million years ago. About 5 million years later, the Dinosauria split into two major groups. The saurischians include all the meat-eaters and the long-necked plant-eaters and the ornithischians were all plant-eaters. The two groups are told apart by the difference in the three large bones of the hip.

In saurischians, the bones point in three directions.

In ornithischians, the lower front bone has swung back.

Tyrannosaurus
The most famous dinosaur. *Tyrannosaurus* from North America fed on plant-eating dinosaurs. At 14 metres long, and with a gape of nearly 1 metre, *Tyrannosaurus* was a fearsome predator.

Who found Dinosaurs?

DINOSAURS WERE FIRST found hundreds of years ago. But these extinct giants have only really been known for less than 200 years. The first dinosaur was named in 1824, and since then hundreds of different species have been discovered in all parts of the world. The story began in Britain and Germany, but by 1870 the most exciting discoveries were coming from North America. After that, the search for dinosaurs spread worldwide, and dozens of huge skeletons came to light in the remotest parts of the world. The search still goes on today. The latest finds have come from Antarctica

THE FIRST DINOSAUR

The first dinosaur that we know about was shown in a book about the natural history of Oxfordshire, England in 1677. A professor at Oxford University wrote about all the strange rocks that had been sent to him, and one of them he recognised as a giant bone. He knew it was from the lower end of a thigh bone (just above the knee), and that it was too big to have come from an elephant. In the end, he thought it came from a giant man or woman!

We now know that this knee bone came from the meat-eating dinosaur *Megalosaurus*. In fact, *Megalosaurus* was the first dinosaur ever to be given a name. More bones had been found over the years, and Professor William Buckland, again of Oxford University, collected them together. He gave it a name in 1824, and *Megalosaurus* means 'big lizard', which is just what he thought it was. Buckland thought that *Megalosaurus* was a huge meat-eating lizard, up to 60 metres (200 feet) long!

Megalosaurus

Megalosaurus (shown below) is now known to have been a large two-legged meat-eating theropod. More complete skeletons have come to light since 1824, and these show much more detail than Buckland could ever have known. Buckland had only a bit of a jaw bone and some other odds and ends from the skeleton to work with.

A thigh bone
The first dinosaur bone ever to be found! This is the lower end of a *Megalosaurus* thigh bone, from just above the knee.

Professor Buckland
William Buckland (1784–1856) was Professor of Geology at Oxford University, and also Dean of Christ Church cathedral there. He was famous not only for studying dinosaurs, but he was also one of the first people to realise that there had been a great Ice Age in the last phase of Earth history.

IGUANA TOOTH

The second dinosaur to be named was *Iguanodon*, a plant-eating form. Some teeth had been found in Sussex, England in 1822, and other bones soon came to light. A local geologist, Gideon Mantell saw that the teeth came from a plant-eater, and he thought it was another giant lizard. *Iguanodon* means 'iguana tooth' since the fossil teeth look a little like the teeth of the modern plant-eating lizards, the iguanas.

Jaw bone
Fragment of jaw bone of *Megalosaurus* showing the large meat-eating teeth: one large tooth stands up on the edge.

Gideon Mantell
Gideon Mantell (1790–1852) was a physician in Lewes, Sussex, who was also a renowned amateur geologist in his spare time. He would hunt for fossils while out on his medical visiting rounds. He wrote some very popular books about geology which sold thousands of copies, and he was one of the first people to make fossil-collecting popular as a hobby. He reported several new dinosaurs from the south of England.

GREAT REPTILES

By 1842, several more dinosaurs had been named from England and from Germany. In that year, Richard Owen, professor of anatomy at the Royal College of Surgeons in London, invented the name 'dinosaur', which means 'fearfully great reptile'. He thought the dinosaurs were not lizards at all, but great rhinoceros-like reptiles. His models can still be seen in Crystal Palace park in south London.

COMPLETE SKELETONS

New finds from North America changed everyone's ideas about the dinosaurs. These new specimens were whole skeletons. The English dinosaurs until then had been just bits and pieces. One of the first skeletons from North America was of *Hadrosaurus*, a duckbilled dinosaur.

From 1870 to 1900, hundreds of dinosaur skeletons were dug up in the American West during the time of the 'bone wars'. Two palaeontologists, Othniel Marsh of Yale University and Edward Cope of Philadelphia, had a race to find more new kinds of dinosaurs than the other. They hated each other, and each spent thousands of dollars to pay workmen to dig as fast as they could.

Hadrosaur skeleton.

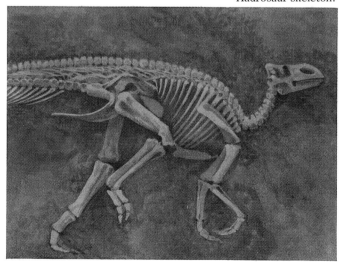

ALL OVER THE WORLD

This century, the search for dinosaurs has gone further afield. Great discoveries have been made in Africa, South America, Mongolia, China, Australia, and India. Only the frozen wastes of Antarctica had never produced a dinosaur, until 1987. Since then, three or more dinosaur skeletons have been found there.

Ankylosaurus
An armoured dinosaur, a group found all over the world.

Where to Find Dinosaurs?

DINOSAURS HAVE BEEN FOUND in all parts of the world, from New York to London, from Russia to Australia, and from Alaska to Antarctica. Most dinosaurs have been found in remote places, a long way from civilization, often in badlands. Badlands are bad for people, because they are often dry and very little can grow but, they are good lands for dinosaurs, because the bare rock comes to the surface, and the wind and rain wash away the soil and rock. This then makes it easy to find bones.

However, some recent discoveries have come from right under the noses of city-dwellers! A spectacular new meat-eating dinosaur with a huge claw, *Baryonyx*, was found in Surrey, not far from London. This was a great surprise, but the best prospect for new finds is to go to unexplored parts of the world where there are rocks the right age.

The Badlands of North America
The first fossil bones were found here about 1850, and since then many hundreds of skeletons have been dug up, and sent to museums all over North America, and to other countries. Desert-like plants grow on top of the plain, and rain water has cut out deep *gulleys* through the earth and rock.

1. Prospecting
Dinosaur hunters *prospect* for bones by marching back and forwards in the Badlands for days on end. When they find some good pieces of bone washed down a stream, they follow them back to the source, and start to dig.

2. Digging
The overburden (rock lying over the skeleton) is removed with picks and shovels, and sometimes even with diggers and pneumatic drills. The dinosaur hunters are much more careful when they get down to the bones!

3. Mapping
The rock is removed carefully from the skeleton using small hand tools. It is important to make a detailed map of how the skeleton is lying in the rock, and to take photographs all the time so that it will be easier to put the skeleton together again in the lab.

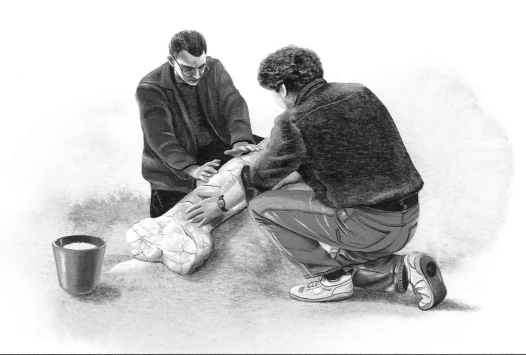

4. Plastering
The bones are carefully cleared, and covered with a jacket of sack-cloth soaked in plaster. Layers of plaster set hard and make a very strong parcel. The packaged bones are carefully removed and loaded up for the trip back to the laboratory.

AT THE MUSEUM
In the museum, the bones have to be taken out of their plaster jackets, cleaned up, and strengthened. The bones may be big, but they are often crumbly. Special glues are used to soak into the *porous* bone and to hold broken pieces together.

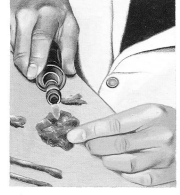

Framing
If a skeleton is mounted for display, it must be held up on a metal or fibreglass frame.

Fitting it together
Putting a dinosaur skeleton together is like solving a *three-dimensional* jigsaw puzzle. The shape of the bones tells the scientist what they are. Missing bones can be made up in plaster.

How Dinosaurs Worked?

THE MAIN JOB of the palaeontologist (a scientist who studies dinosaurs and other fossil animals and plants) is to make the ancient world come to life. How does the palaeontologist make a living animal from a pile of old bones? Can you believe the pictures, stories and films about dinosaurs, or is it all just a scientist's imagination? It is actually possible to work out a great deal from the dinosaur bones, from other fossils of plants and animals, and even from the rocks in which the fossils are found. But the first and most important evidence comes from a very detailed look at the dinosaur bones.

LOOKING AT BONES

When the bones have been cleaned up and strengthened, they are laid out in the lab so that they can be identified. It may be possible to fit some of them together, like the separate bones of the backbone (the vertebrae) which lock together closely. The palaeontologists will try to identify the dinosaur by comparing their new bones with *specimens* found before, and with drawings of bones that have been published in scientific journals.

PUTTING FLESH ON THE BONES

The fossils are only the hard parts of the dinosaur, its skeleton. How can a palaeontologist put the flesh back on as well? Flesh, the meat you eat, is mainly muscle. Muscles are there to make parts of the body move, and they are all fixed on to bones at each end. Ancient dinosaur bones give clues about dinosaur flesh. There are often clear marks where the muscles used to be.

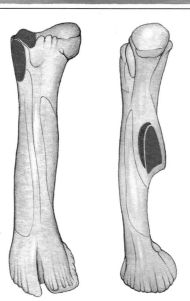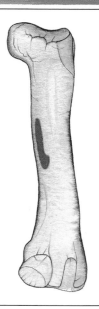

Shaded areas are where muscles attach

TESTING JOINTS

How much could a dinosaur bend its arm, leg, or neck? If the bones are well preserved, the palaeontologist can fit the joints together and find out. The bones of the hip, knee, and ankle joints, for example, can show exactly how a dinosaur moved its hind leg. Here are three different joints that allow a varying amount of movement.

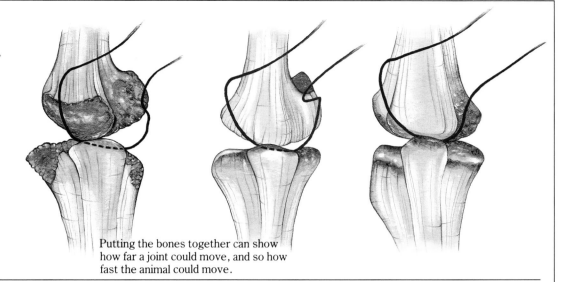

Putting the bones together can show how far a joint could move, and so how fast the animal could move.

HOW HEAVY?

Some of the long-necked plant-eating dinosaurs were the biggest land animals of all time. But how big were they? Palaeontologists can work out how heavy a dinosaur was if they make a detailed model of the animal with its flesh. The heaviest ones, like *Brachiosaurus*, could reach 50 tonnes. If a dinosaur was heavier than 100 tonnes or so, its legs would have been so fat that it could not have walked!

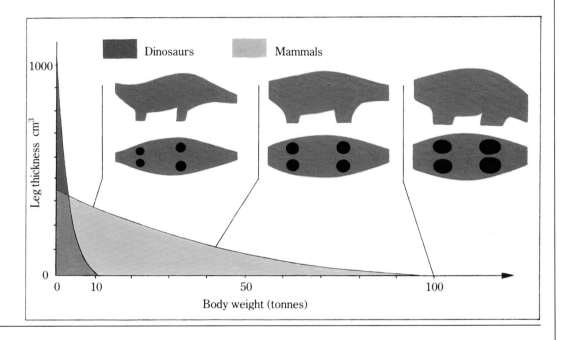

MUSCLES

The final piece of evidence is to look at modern animals. Palaeontologists might compare the leg of a dinosaur with a crocodile or a bird to see where the muscles went. All backboned animals have roughly the same muscles, and it is likely that dinosaurs had these also. Our biceps muscle bends our arm up and it is just the same in a gorilla, a lizard, and a dinosaur.

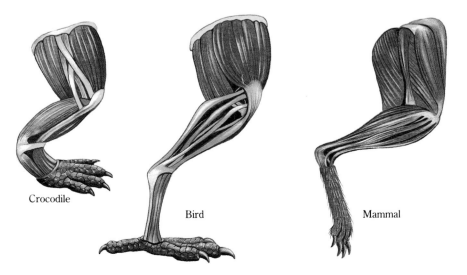

Crocodile

Bird

Mammal

How Dinosaurs Worked II?

WHEN THE MUSCLES have been put back on a dinosaur skeleton, can we understand any more about how that dinosaur lived? How fast could it run, what did it eat, what noises did it make, what colour was it? These questions are tackled later in the book. But, first, the whole animal has to be understood. And a clear model or picture has to be made to show the living dinosaur in a scene of other animals and plants that it saw when it walked around millions of years ago.

HOW MUSCLES WORK

Muscles pull on bones. Muscles cannot push. This means that there are many different muscles around an arm and a leg, so that these limbs can move in different ways.

Triceratops

This was a four-legged rhinoceros-like plant-eater. It had powerful legs, and could have trotted fast, but not run as fast as a smaller animal, such as a horse or deer. The heavy bones supported large leg muscles.

Cerartosaurus

This was a two-legged meat-eater which could run fast when it was chasing its prey. It had strong muscles on its legs, like an ostrich or human being.

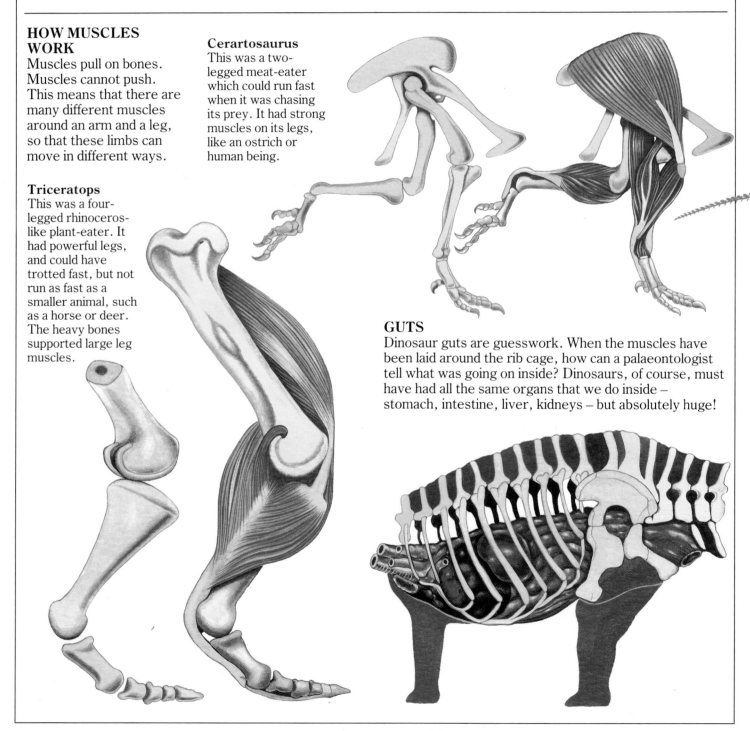

GUTS

Dinosaur guts are guesswork. When the muscles have been laid around the rib cage, how can a palaeontologist tell what was going on inside? Dinosaurs, of course, must have had all the same organs that we do inside – stomach, intestine, liver, kidneys – but absolutely huge!

PUTTING IT ALL TOGETHER

The guts may be guesswork, but the flesh and bones are not. Palaeontologists can be quite confident about the shape of a dinosaur, if the skeleton is good enough, and about its muscles.

Bones

The skeleton is strung together, and all the joints tested carefully. The pose of the body is based on the close study of the bone joints, and on comparisons with large living animals.

Muscles

The muscles are laid on layer by layer after a study of muscle scars on the bones. The scars tell us where the muscles fitted on, and roughly how large they were.

Skin

The other soft parts are more difficult to reconstruct. The skin is then laid over the whole body, but this is one of the most difficult parts. What colour was the skin?

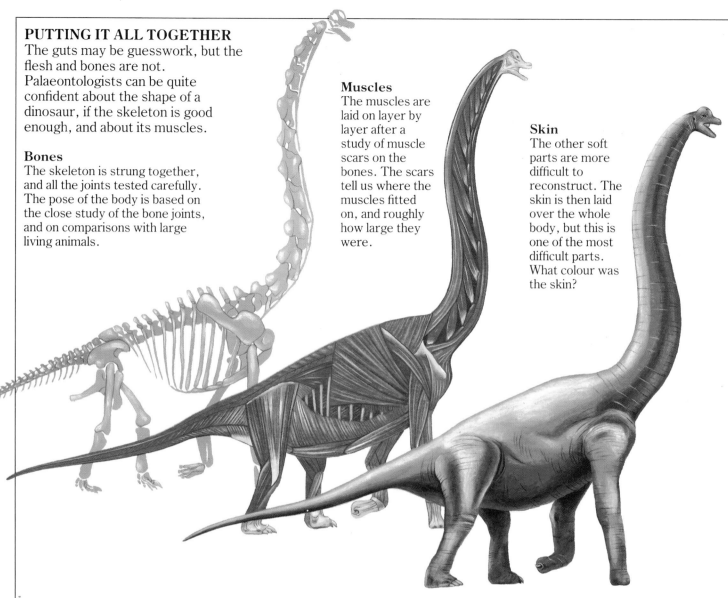

MAKING A MODEL

Models of reconstructed dinosaurs are made for display in museums. The models are made smaller than the real thing, of course, and they may take weeks of careful scientific study, and artistic work to put together. Sometimes these detailed models may be made in plastic so that everyone can buy one. Of course, most plastic dinosaur models are not so good!

You can measure the volume of a model dinosaur by filling a glass full of water. Lower the dinosaur into the glass and catch the water that spills over the edge. The weight of this water will give you the volume of the dinosaur.

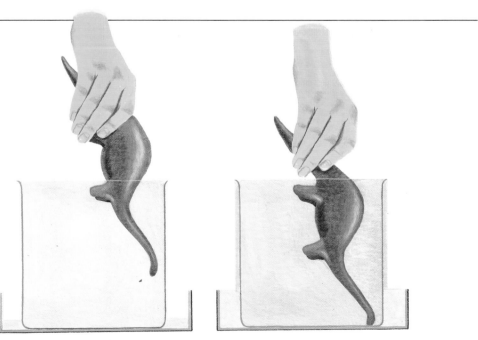

What Colour They Were?

NO-ONE HAS EVER found a fossil which shows the colour of a dinosaur. Surprisingly, there are quite a few specimens of dinosaur skin, at least moulds of the skin pressed into the rock beside a skeleton. Usually, of course, the skin and flesh rot away completely. But, in some cases, dinosaurs seem to have been *mummified*, because the soft parts dried out under the hot sun, and the whole body was buried. Eventually, the flesh rotted away, but an impression of the skin may survive. These skin fossils show that most dinosaurs had scales of some sort. Many dinosaurs also had quite thick plates of bone set into their skin, as crocodiles do today, to give protection.

Can we know?
What colour were the big sauropods, such as *Apatosaurus*, green, brown, blue, purple with orange spots? We shall never know.

Grey or brown
The sauropods may have been dull grey or brown. Many very large animals today, such as elephants, hippos, and rhinos are grey, which may help them control their body temperatures.

Mottled

Another possibility is that *Apatosaurus* was greenish or mottled. This would have been a kind of camouflage that blended in with the trees and open plains where he lived. But why be camouflaged when you are so big that you have no fear of *predators*?

WHY ARE ANIMALS COLOURED?

Camouflage

Many animals today are camouflaged. Their colours match the background, and this makes them hard to see. This can be useful for plant-eaters or meat-eaters since it allows them to hide.

Warning

Some animals have warning colours. Some snakes and lizards, for example, are coloured with bright reds, yellows, and blacks. This tells big predators 'keep off, I bite'. A bird may try to eat a snake once, but will never try again!

Temperature control

Colour may be involved in temperature control. In hot climates, many large animals are dull grey or brown so that they do not take in heat from the sun. This may have been true also of the larger dinosaurs.

Advertising

Colour may also be used to give messages to other animals of the same species. Many male birds are brightly coloured as a kind of advertisement to the females. The colours say 'look how splendid and smart I am. I will be a good father for your children'.

How Long Ago They Lived?

THE EARTH IS VERY OLD. It formed about 4600 million years ago. The first living things appeared about 3500 million years ago, and humans only came on the scene about 5 million years ago. How do palaeontologists know these ages? Is it just guesswork? The answers come from geologists, who are the scientists who study the history of the Earth, and they can work out these ages from the record of the rocks. There are great thicknesses of rocks which can be seen in *quarries*, in cliffs, and even in deep boreholes drilled through the Earth's crust. The order of the layers of rocks, the fossils found in the rocks, and *radioactive chemicals* can all give evidence of age.

DATING THE FOSSILS

When geologists look at the order of the rocks, from very old ones to younger ones, they can see that the fossils are in some sort of order too. The oldest rocks have no fossils, then simple single-celled creatures, then sponges and corals, then shellfish, then fishes, and so on.

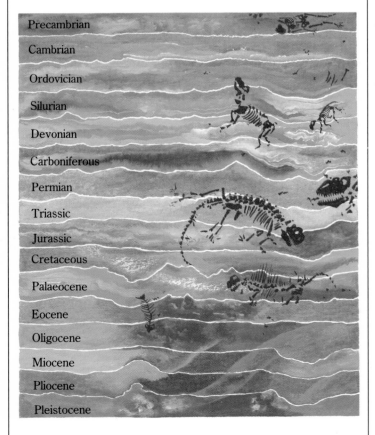

Precambrian
Cambrian
Ordovician
Silurian
Devonian
Carboniferous
Permian
Triassic
Jurassic
Cretaceous
Palaeocene
Eocene
Oligocene
Miocene
Pliocene
Pleistocene

A SWEEP OF TIME

The diagram below shows the great sweep of geological time, running from the origin of the Earth to the present day. Dinosaurs appeared late in the story, but still long, long before the first humans.

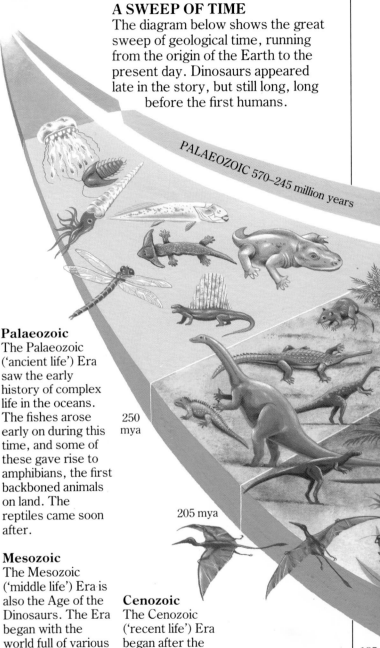

PALAEOZOIC 570–245 million years

250 mya

205 mya

135 mya

Palaeozoic
The Palaeozoic ('ancient life') Era saw the early history of complex life in the oceans. The fishes arose early on during this time, and some of these gave rise to amphibians, the first backboned animals on land. The reptiles came soon after.

Mesozoic
The Mesozoic ('middle life') Era is also the Age of the Dinosaurs. The Era began with the world full of various kinds of reptiles, and the dinosaurs arose about 20 million years after the beginning of the Era. Later, came the crocodiles, lizards, snakes, turtles, birds, and mammals.

Cenozoic
The Cenozoic ('recent life') Era began after the great extinction of the dinosaurs, and of many other Mesozoic groups on land and in the sea. The scene became dominated by mammals on land. The latest major mammal group to appear were humans, at most 5 million years ago.

HOW ANIMALS TURN TO STONE

Fossils are the remains of plants and animals that once lived. Usually, fossils are the hard parts of those ancient creatures, like bones or shells with all the spaces filled up with rock. In bone there are many internal cavities which contain blood vessels, *nerves*, marrow tissue, and fat which rot away soon after the animal has died. If the bone is buried, these spaces may fill partly with sand or mud. Later on, the bone may be buried very deep and waters containing minerals may pass through. Some of these minerals may also be formed inside the bone as crystals.

1. Dying
An animal – here an ichthyosaur – falls to the bottom of the sea when it dies. Scavenging animals may eat its flesh.

2. Rotting
Most of the flesh may be eaten, or it may rot away. Usually only the hard parts of the bony skeleton are left behind.

3. Buried
Over a relatively short time, mud and sand may be dumped on top of the skeleton, progressively burying it.

4. Fossil Skeleton
Millions of years later, the ancient sea floor may have become dry land, and a palaeontologist may find the skeleton.

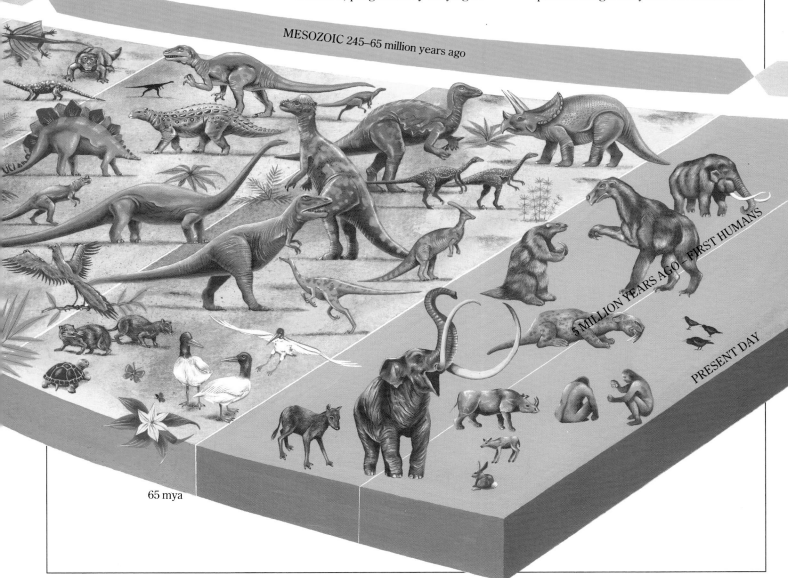

MESOZOIC 245–65 million years ago

5 MILLION YEARS AGO – FIRST HUMANS

PRESENT DAY

65 mya

Where They Came From?

DINOSAURS DID NOT spring onto the Earth from nowhere. Nor were they the first and only great extinct animals of all time. A long history of the *evolution* of life is known before the dinosaurs came on the scene, indeed over 3000 million years of evolution! Dinosaurs are vertebrates – animals with backbones, just like us – and the first vertebrates were simple fish-like animals that lived about 500 million years ago. The first land vertebrates were *amphibians* which came on to land about 375 million years ago. Then came the reptiles. It was about 225 million years ago that the first dinosaurs appeared.

EVOLUTION OF THE DINOSAURS

The oldest dinosaurs date from the Santa Maria Formation (opposite), 225 million years ago. They were small two-legged meat-eaters. The dinosaurs originated from among the archosaurs, a group that came to prominence during the Triassic Period and included some plant-eaters, but mainly meat-eaters. Three or four main lines of dinosaur evolution became established during the Late Triassic.

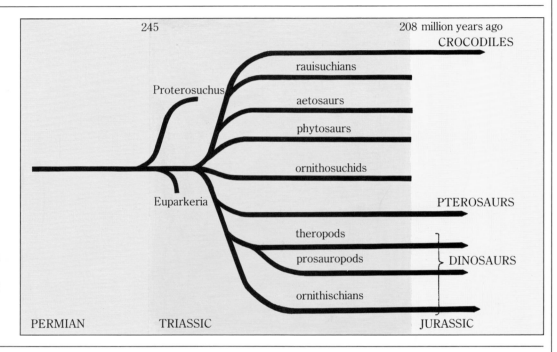

245   208 million years ago

CROCODILES

rauisuchians

Proterosuchus

aetosaurs

phytosaurs

ornithosuchids

Euparkeria

PTEROSAURS

theropods

prosauropods

} DINOSAURS

ornithischians

PERMIAN   TRIASSIC   JURASSIC

AGE OF MAMMAL-LIKE REPTILES

The first reptiles were small animals. They laid eggs on land and could get away from the water, unlike the amphibians which laid their eggs in water. The first 100 million years of reptile evolution were dominated by the mammal-like reptiles, small and large plant- and meat-eaters. These were true reptiles (they laid eggs and had scaly skins), but they showed mammal-like teeth. Reptiles have teeth which are all the same from back to front of the jaws, but mammals, and many mammal-like reptiles, had different sorts of teeth. The mammal-like reptiles were hugely successful.

Lycaenops
This was an advanced meat-eating mammal-like reptile of the Late Permian. It had long canine teeth for piercing prey.

Dimetrodon
This was a famous sail-backed reptile of the Early Permian. The sail may have helped control its body heat.

SANTA MARIA SCENE

A scene in Brazil during the Late Triassic, 225 million years ago, marks a turning point in the history of life on Earth. Most of the animals were mammal-like reptiles, such as *Dinodontosaurus*, or other less familiar forms such as *Scaphonyx*. A small two-legged meat-eater, *Herrerasaurus*, might not have seemed important. This kind of scene was all over the world at the time – during the Triassic all the continents were joined together, and the animals could move freely anywhere. Not long after, most of these creatures had died out, and the dinosaurs took over.

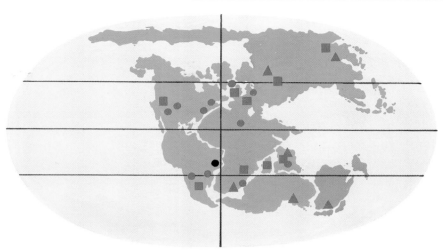

The world 225 million years ago, at the beginning of the age of the dinosaurs.

1. Plant-eater
Scaphonyx was a plant-eating rhynchosaur ('snouted reptile') an odd-looking animal, but the commonest creature of its day.

2. The first dinosaur
Herrerasaurus, the first dinosaur, was rather rare – only two or three skeletons are known, but it is the first dinosaur.

3. Mammal-like reptile
Dinodontosaurus, one of the last of the mammal-like reptiles.

But this was not the end of these reptiles – distant relatives were slowly evolving into true mammals.

Where They Lived?

HOW DO WE KNOW about the world of the dinosaurs? Did they live in steaming *tropical jungles*, or blasted sandy deserts? Are the scenes in books and films imaginary? The evidence comes from the rocks. Dinosaur bones are never found on their own. They are usually buried in sandstones or mudstones that tell a story to the geologists who study the sites. There may be evidence of an ancient river. There may be tree stumps, branches and leaves that tell about the plants the dinosaurs may have fed on. There may be fossils of other animals – insects, fishes, turtles, crocodiles – that complete the scene.

AN ANCIENT LANDSCAPE
The scene shown here is a detailed reconstruction of life during the Early Cretaceous in southern England, 125 million years ago. It is based on dozens of dinosaur digs, over the past 150 million years, in the Wealden rocks of Kent, Sussex, Surrey, and the Isle of Wight.

The hills were covered with conifer trees – ancestors of pines and spruces.

Dinosaurs like the plant-eater *Iguanodon* lived on the lowlands, and fed on leaves from the trees.

Plants
Leaves, stems, twigs, tree trunks, and roots show that there were all kinds of plants present, from waterside horsetails and ferns, to ginkgo, cycad, and conifer trees.

Fern frond

Pollen grain covered with small plates

Spores and pollen
In some places, whole plants are not found, but fossil pollen and spores can be used to identify the types. Indeed, pollen and spores can be very useful in giving an idea of the relative importance of the different plant types.

Dinosaur bones may be found in river and lake sands and muds. The bones may be arranged as skeletons or washed along and scattered.

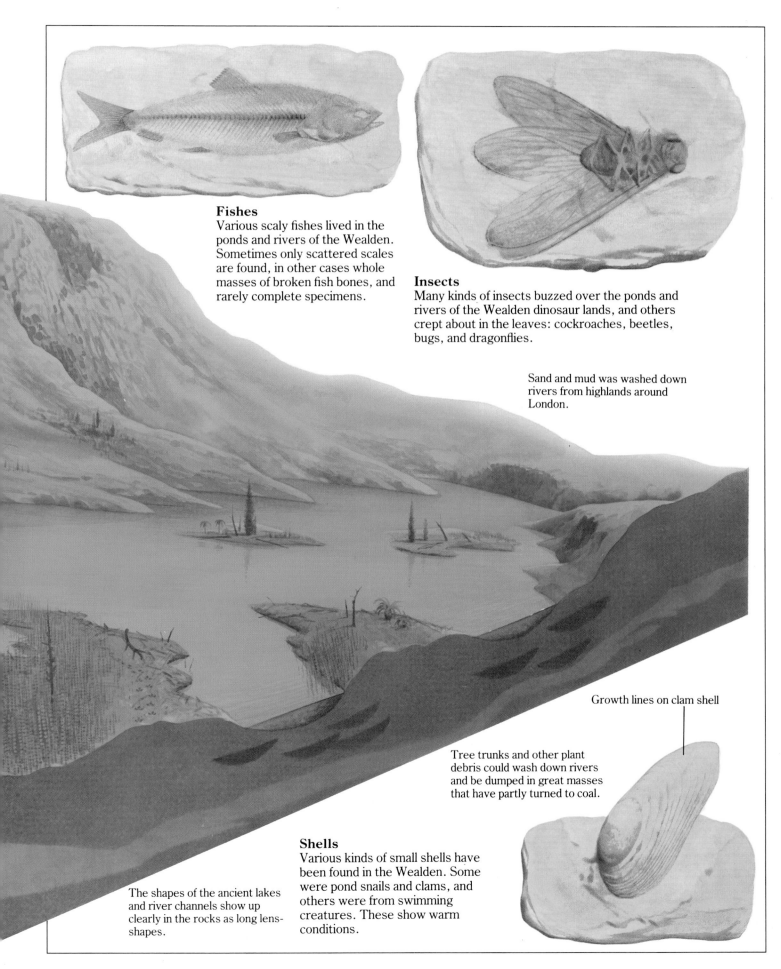

Fishes
Various scaly fishes lived in the ponds and rivers of the Wealden. Sometimes only scattered scales are found, in other cases whole masses of broken fish bones, and rarely complete specimens.

Insects
Many kinds of insects buzzed over the ponds and rivers of the Wealden dinosaur lands, and others crept about in the leaves: cockroaches, beetles, bugs, and dragonflies.

Sand and mud was washed down rivers from highlands around London.

Growth lines on clam shell

Tree trunks and other plant debris could wash down rivers and be dumped in great masses that have partly turned to coal.

Shells
Various kinds of small shells have been found in the Wealden. Some were pond snails and clams, and others were from swimming creatures. These show warm conditions.

The shapes of the ancient lakes and river channels show up clearly in the rocks as long lens-shapes.

What They Ate?

DINOSAURS DIETS WERE as varied as were dinosaur sizes. Some small dinosaurs ate insects and worms, while Tyrannosaurs fed on other large dinosaurs. Among plant-eaters, there were some dinosaurs that could eat only soft leaves, while others could eat tough pine needles. Other dinosaurs may have fed on fruit or roots, while some probably specialised on a diet of fish. Some forms, such as Oviraptor from Mongolia, had no teeth and may have fed on eggs.

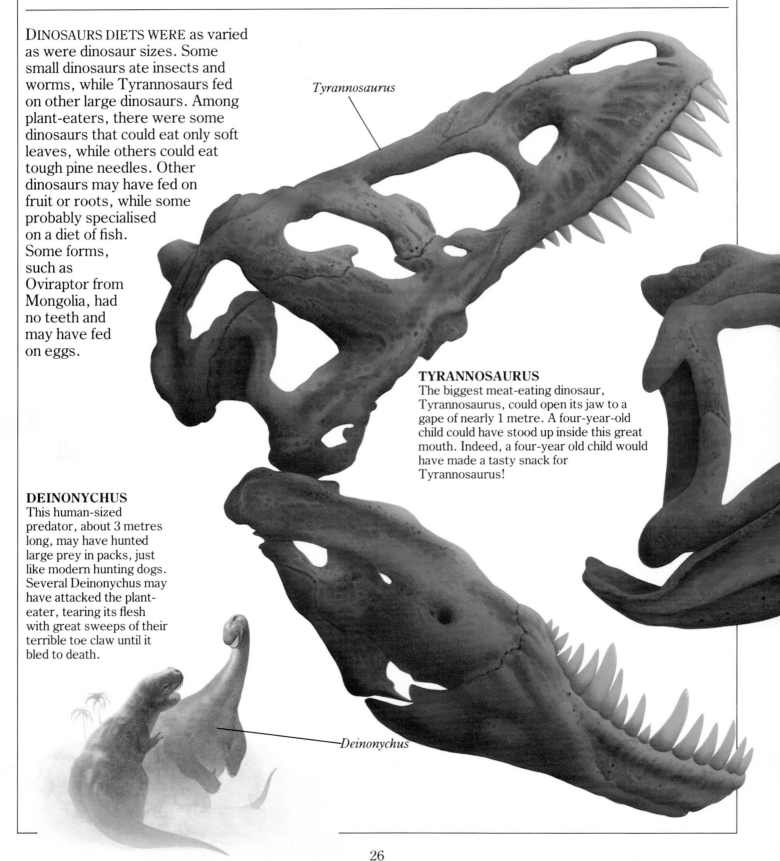

Tyrannosaurus

TYRANNOSAURUS
The biggest meat-eating dinosaur, Tyrannosaurus, could open its jaw to a gape of nearly 1 metre. A four-year-old child could have stood up inside this great mouth. Indeed, a four-year old child would have made a tasty snack for Tyrannosaurus!

DEINONYCHUS
This human-sized predator, about 3 metres long, may have hunted large prey in packs, just like modern hunting dogs. Several Deinonychus may have attacked the plant-eater, tearing its flesh with great sweeps of their terrible toe claw until it bled to death.

Deinonychus

PROBLEMS OF PLANT-EATING

The most successful plant-eating dinosaurs were the ornithopods, two-legged forms such as Iguanodon and the duckbills. They were even able to chew their food, something no other reptile can do. The ornithopods could not move their jaws around as we can. In some early forms (1), the lower jaws moved in as the jaws closed. In others (2), the sides of the skull flapped out as the jaws closed.

DIGESTIVE SYSTEM

Ornithopods could chew, and so cut their food up a little. Other dinosaurs, like all reptiles today, swallowed their food whole and might have had horrible tummy trouble. However, they probably had large muscular stomachs which squeezed the food, and which contained acids to break it up. Plant-eating dinosaurs probably also swallowed grit to help grind their food.

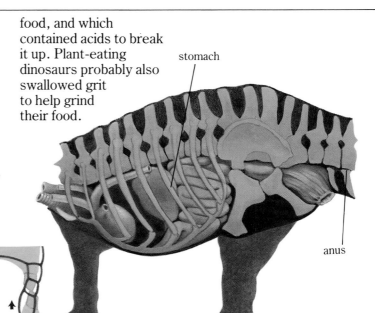

stomach

anus

PLATEOSAURUS SKULL

The shape of this skull is quite different from the meat-eating Tyrannosaurus skull. The jaw joint, at the back, is set low, and the back part of the jaw is deep. Together, these show that there were powerful jaw muscles and a powerful bite near the back of the tooth row, both necessary for cutting tough plants. Stems and leaves could be gathered into the horse-like skull and cut up along the length of the jaws.

TEETH

Meat-eaters all have flattened, curved, pointed teeth with zig-zag edges, all designed to saw up meat and bone. The teeth curve back in the jaws in order to stop the prey from escaping. Plant-eating dinosaurs had a range of 'leaf-shaped' teeth, usually quite broad and flat, often ridged, and often with coarse zig-zag edges.

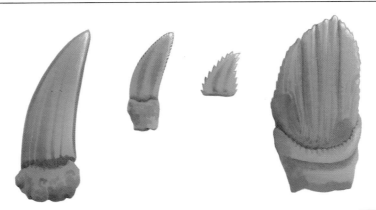

If Dinosaurs Slept?

DID DINOSAURS SLEEP, like dogs, cats, and humans, or were they awake all the time, like most animals? Did dinosaurs go out to feed during the day or at night? Were they *warm-blooded* or not? These are some of the most difficult questions to answer since it is hard to know how to begin to find out. However, palaeontologists can make some sensible guesses based on modern animals. And, there are a surprising number of ways of looking at the question of body temperature.

Kamptobaatar
Early mammals lived side by side with the dinosaurs. In fact, mammals had arisen not long after the dinosaurs (see page 21). They had hair, were warm-blooded and probably fed at night.

Tarbosaurus
The great dinosaurs probably slept at night: maybe not the deep sleep that humans need, but the sleep of a cold-blooded animal. As the air became colder, the large dinosaurs may simply have slowed down.

BODY TEMPERATURE

Cold-blooded animals like lizards and snakes are not always cold. Their body temperature is usually the same as the air temperature, so they can be very hot on a hot day! Warm-blooded animals, like humans, keep the same body temperature all the time, whether the air is hot or cold. Large cold-blooded animals (like big crocodiles) are somewhere in between. They take so long to warm up and so long to cool down that their body temperature actually stays fairly constant even when nights are cold and days are very hot.

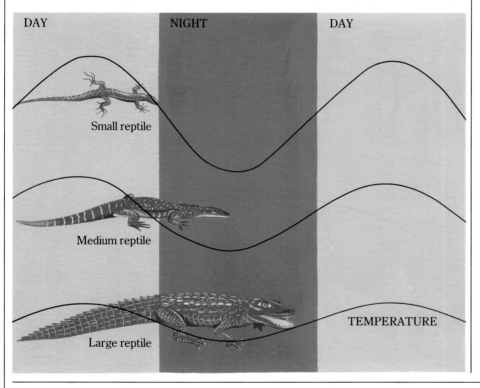

DAY | NIGHT | DAY

Small reptile

Medium reptile

Large reptile

TEMPERATURE

BONE STRUCTURE

In 1975, several palaeontologists noticed that dinosaur bone looked very like mammal bone when it was cut into slices and examined under the microscope. It did not seem to be anything like the bone structure of a cold-blooded lizard. It turns out, however, that all large animals have the 'mammal' type of bone, and small animals have the 'lizard' type.

Lizard bone

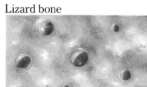

Dinosaur bone

Blood vessel canal

Cow bone

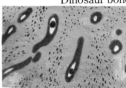

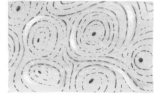

Stegosaurus

This plated dinosaur gives clues about dinosaur body heat. What were the great plates for along the middle of the back of *Stegosaurus*? They stood up too high to be much use in protecting the body from meat-eaters. They were covered with blood vessels, and must have worked like radiators. Experiments with a metal *Stegosaurus* in a wind tunnel showed how the plates were perfect for taking up heat and giving heat off.

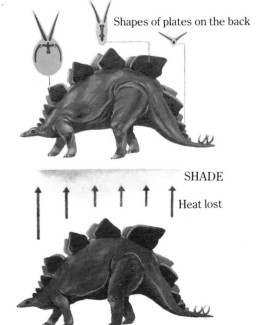

Shapes of plates on the back

SUN

Heat taken in

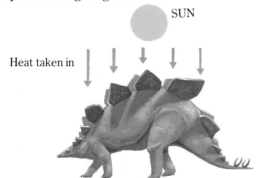

SHADE

Heat lost

Heating
Early in the morning, *Stegosaurus* could stand sideways to the sun, and heat would be absorbed through the plates, and passed into the body through the *blood stream*.

Cooling
Later on, when the noonday sun became too hot, *Stegosaurus* could find some shade, or stand in a breeze, and heat would have been radiated from the plates.

If They Could Run?

HOW FAST could the fastest dinosaur run? How can we measure dinosaur speeds? A great deal can be worked out about dinosaurs walking and running. The bones of the legs can be studied, and the joints can be worked to see just how the legs could move. The leg muscles can be restored layer by layer, and even the strengths of those muscles can be worked out (the fatter a muscle is, the stronger it is). The shape of a dinosaur's leg bones and muscles can be compared with modern animals – horses, humans, rhinos, elephants, ostriches – to find how that dinosaur could run. Most amazingly, recent studies of dinosaur footprints have shown that these can give exact readings of running speeds.

FAST AND SLOW

The slowest dinosaurs moved at 1–2 km per hour (1 mile per hour or less), which is slower than human walking speed. Most of them seem to have walked at about the speed of a grown-up human who is in a hurry, which is about 5–6 km per hour, or 3–4 miles per hour.

Running at speed

The running styles of an ostrich dinosaur, based on film of a moving modern ostrich, which is a flightless bird with the same build. It could run at the same speed as a galloping race horse.

TRACKS

Fossil dinosaur footprints and trackways are very common in all parts of the world. They used to be seen as just another interesting piece of evidence for the shape of dinosaurs' feet. Footprints can show the exact shape of the flesh of the foot, claws, and even skin patterns. They also tell us dinosaur speeds. A simple equation, worked out in 1976, shows that the speed is in proportion to the stride length (the spacing of the footprints).

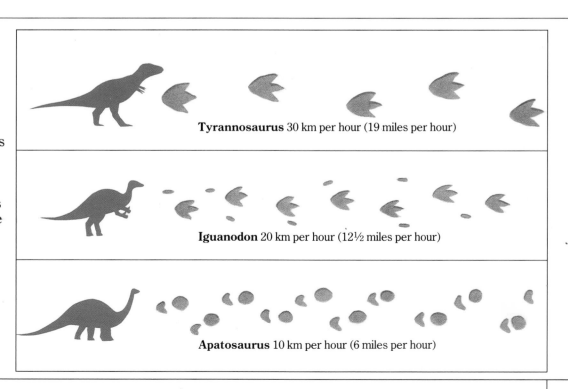

Tyrannosaurus 30 km per hour (19 miles per hour)

Iguanodon 20 km per hour (12½ miles per hour)

Apatosaurus 10 km per hour (6 miles per hour)

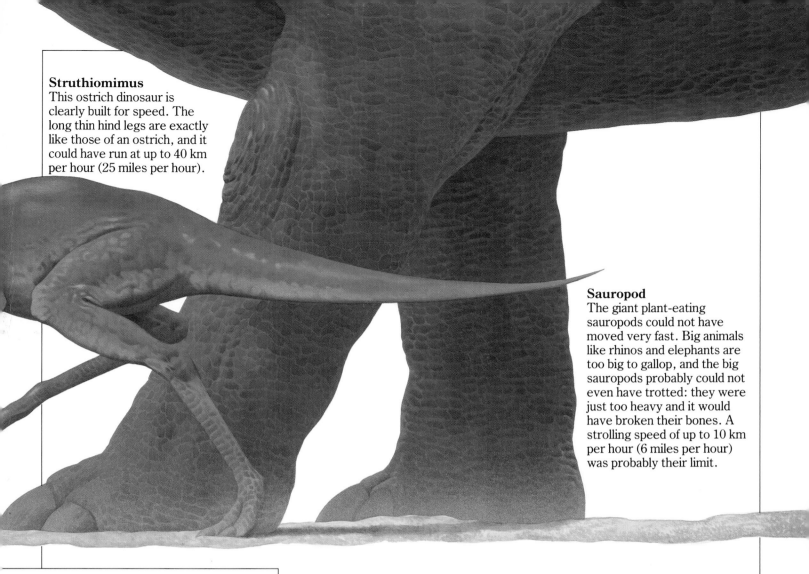

Struthiomimus
This ostrich dinosaur is clearly built for speed. The long thin hind legs are exactly like those of an ostrich, and it could have run at up to 40 km per hour (25 miles per hour).

Sauropod
The giant plant-eating sauropods could not have moved very fast. Big animals like rhinos and elephants are too big to gallop, and the big sauropods probably could not even have trotted: they were just too heavy and it would have broken their bones. A strolling speed of up to 10 km per hour (6 miles per hour) was probably their limit.

Modern comparisons
Tracks of modern animals have helped palaeontologists to study dinosaur tracks, which can reveal how they walked and ran.

| Lizard | Bird | Mammal |

COMPARING SPEEDS
Large heavy animals can only walk. Slightly smaller animals, like rhinos can trot, which is just a kind of fast walking. Medium-sized animals, such as horses and dogs, can gallop, which is a very fast way to move. Fastest of all are cheetahs, which can reach speeds of 112 km per hour (70 miles per hour). There were probably no dinosaurs as fast as that!

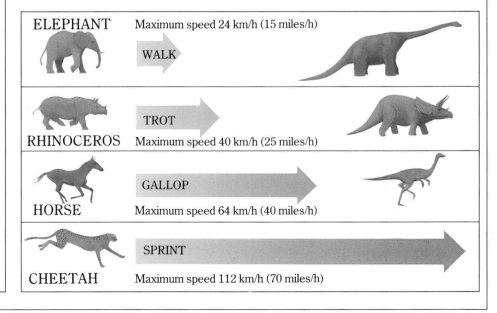

ELEPHANT — Maximum speed 24 km/h (15 miles/h) — WALK

RHINOCEROS — Maximum speed 40 km/h (25 miles/h) — TROT

HORSE — Maximum speed 64 km/h (40 miles/h) — GALLOP

CHEETAH — Maximum speed 112 km/h (70 miles/h) — SPRINT

Whether They Could Swim?

MOST ANIMALS CAN SWIM, even if some, like cats, do not like it! At one time, palaeontologists thought that only the large sauropods could swim, and that duckbilled dinosaurs could swim using a kind of built-in *snorkel*. They believed that these plant-eaters kept well out in the middle of lakes to escape from meat-eating dinosaurs. There are many reasons why these ideas are wrong. There is proof that the meat-eaters could swim. The sauropods would have died if they had lived in deep lakes and duckbills did not have snorkels, but trumpet-like chests (see page 35).

OLD AND NEW VIEWS

The large plant-eating sauropods certainly lived round lakes some of the time. But it is most unlikely that they stood in the middle of deep lakes, using their long necks to detect danger. A dangerous scientific experiment showed why. As the water becomes deeper, the pressure becomes higher, and it is impossible to breathe. Below 2–3 metres, the sauropod could not breathe in.

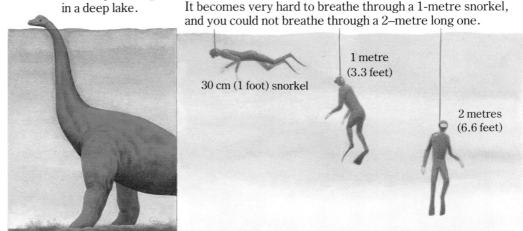

Wrong View
A sauropod living in a deep lake.

The experiment
Humans can breathe through a 30-centimetre long snorkel. It becomes very hard to breathe through a 1-metre snorkel, and you could not breathe through a 2–metre long one.

30 cm (1 foot) snorkel

1 metre (3.3 feet)

2 metres (6.6 feet)

COULD MEAT-EATERS SWIM?

The old idea was that a fierce meat-eating dinosaur would chase a herd of plant-eaters down to the waterside. They would jump in and swim away to safety and the meat-eater would be left on the bank growling and snarling in rage. This is nonsense of course, and the evidence to prove it wrong was found in the 1980s: a trackway of a swimming *Megalosaurus*.

Meat-eaters track
The trackway above showed that meat-eaters could swim. While his body floated, *Megalosaurus* stroked himself along with delicate kicks on the bottom of an ancient lake.

SAUROPOD SWIMMING

The great sauropods could swim as well as any other dinosaur, but they did it with their necks stretched out straight in front. In this position, the lungs (inside the chest) were just below the surface, and the dinosaur could breathe easily. Some fossil trackways show the sauropods padding themselves along in the water with just their feet touching the bottom.

If Dinosaurs Could Think?

DINOSAURS ARE OFTEN SAID to have been very stupid. They were huge, but had tiny brains. This means that they could not have thought about very much and this is often said to be the reason why they died out. Of course, when palaeontologists look more closely at the evidence by studying the sizes of dinosaurs' brains, the story is not so simple at all. In fact, most dinosaurs were just as intelligent, or just as stupid, as modern reptiles. Some dinosaurs were actually as clever as birds.

BRAINS

Dinosaur brains can sometimes be studied in detail. The brain fitted tightly into a space in the back of the skull, and the bones that wrapped round the brain to protect it actually show its exact shape. It is possible to look at a cast from the inside of the braincase which shows the exact shape of the dinosaur's brain.

Brain cast

This brain cast from *Tyrannosaurus* (above) is a long sausage-shaped object, really very small compared to the size of the animal. The lumps and blobs in the brain are the different parts, connected with hearing, sight, smell, balance, and so on. Many nerves pass out of the side of the brain and help to operate the mouth, the eyes, ears, and other parts.

Braincase

Saurornithoides had a bird-sized brain. This intelligent dinosaur had a large braincase, and its brain was much larger in proportion to its body size than the brain of most dinosaurs. The biggest parts of the brain were for vision and for balance, since *Saurornithoides* led a very active life.

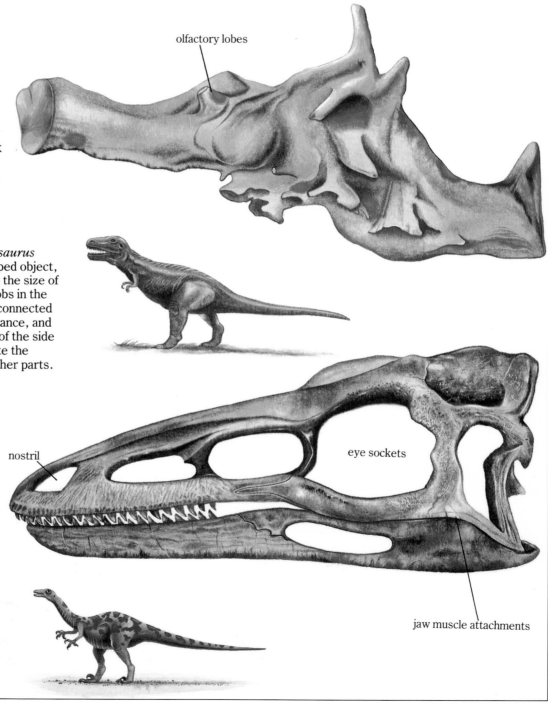

olfactory lobes

nostril

eye sockets

jaw muscle attachments

COMPARING BRAIN SIZES

Weight for weight, mammals such as ourselves have larger brains than birds, and birds have larger brains than reptiles and most dinosaurs. The important thing is to remember that actual brain size is not a good guide to intelligence. After all, elephants have bigger brains than humans. What is important is the relative brain size, in proportion to body size. Humans have very high relative brain sizes, dinosaurs have very small relative brain sizes.

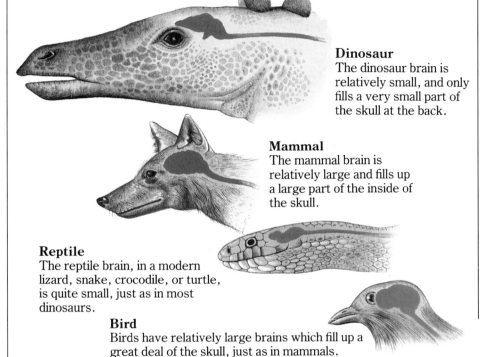

Dinosaur
The dinosaur brain is relatively small, and only fills a very small part of the skull at the back.

Mammal
The mammal brain is relatively large and fills up a large part of the inside of the skull.

Reptile
The reptile brain, in a modern lizard, snake, crocodile, or turtle, is quite small, just as in most dinosaurs.

Bird
Birds have relatively large brains which fill up a great deal of the skull, just as in mammals.

ADAPTING

One scientist thought that dinosaurs were so stupid that they could not have learnt from their mistakes. They would keep on banging their heads on branches, falling over stones, and eating poisonous plants. This is not likely, however. Dinosaurs were very successful animals, and they were no more stupid than a living crocodile.

DUCKBILLS

Evidence that dinosaurs were not all stupid comes from the duckbills. They could tell each other apart by looking at their faces, just as humans do, and they could do this also by listening to their voices. The crests on top of the duckbills' heads were different in males and females, and different in young ones. Also, each species had a different crest.

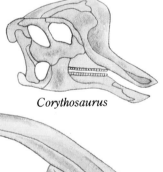

Corythosaurus

Parasaurolophus male

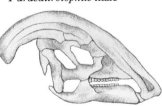

Parasaurolophus female

A hollow crest
The crest was hollow and carried the breathing tubes inside. When it breathed out, the duckbill made a great honking noise. Different-shaped crests made different honks, so every dinosaur had a different voice.

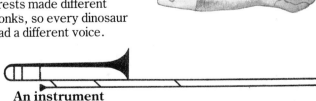

An instrument
The curves and loops in the breathing tubes of a duckbill are just like the curves in a trombone.

An orchestra!
Different instruments sound different. Experiments with duckbill skulls sound like an ancient orchestra!

How Dinosaurs Bred?

REPTILES LAY EGGS, just as birds do. However, modern reptiles usually lay their eggs on the ground, or buried in sand. Dinosaurs also laid eggs, and dinosaur nests have been known for some time. The first dinosaur nests were found about 1925 in Mongolia. But it is only recently that palaeontologists have studied dinosaur nests in detail. It turns out that dinosaurs may even have sat on their nests, and protected the eggs. They also helped the new-born babies by bringing them food. As far as we can tell, dinosaurs were good parents.

SIZE OF EGGS

Many dinosaurs were huge, and it might seem obvious that they must have laid huge eggs. This is not the case, however. The biggest dinosaur eggs were about 30 centimetres (one foot) long, the same size as the biggest birds' eggs. The reason that big dinosaurs did not lay huge eggs is that the young had to be able to get out. The bigger an egg is, the thicker its shell has to be, or it might collapse. If the shell is too thick, the baby cannot get out.

Ostrich
The biggest eggs today are laid by ostriches, and extinct flightless birds laid even larger ones, up to 30 centimetres (1 foot) long.

Turkey
Turkeys lay medium-sized eggs, in proportion to their body size, and much bigger than a common hen's egg.

Hen
A hen's egg is still larger than the eggs of many smaller birds and reptiles.

DINOSAUR NESTS

The new work in Montana, USA, shows that dinosaur mothers came back year after year to the same nesting site. Palaeontologists have dug down through layers of rock, and they have found dinosaur nests one on top of the other: the nests were dug out each year, then covered by flood waters carrying sand and mud, and then new nests were dug on top in the following year.

Sites
This diagram shows layers of rock separated to show the nest sites in similar places year after year.

DINOSAUR EGGS

Inside the egg, the embryo gets larger, until it is big enough to hatch out. The embryo feeds on a special high-protein food that is inside the egg, namely the yolk, and there is even a special bag for unwanted waste products.

Fossil egg
Dinosaur eggs were covered with a hard shell, rather like the shell of a hen's egg. In dinosaurs, this shell often had a knobbly pattern on the outside. Fossil specimens are often crushed.

yolk sac

hard egg shell

waste bag

HOW DINOSAURS MADE NESTS

The new work in Montana has shown in some detail how dinosaurs built their nests. The nests were made by a duckbilled dinosaur called *Maiasaura* ("good mother reptile") and a plant-eating relative of *Hypsilophodon* called *Orodromeus*. Hundreds of nests have been found at a site which has been renamed 'Egg Mountain'.

The favourite nesting site seems to have been on an island. The site is surrounded by rocks laid down in lake waters, and it rises above these layers. Perhaps this site was safer for the nests, and away from some of the animals that might have tried to eat the eggs.

Hatching
Babies hatched out of their eggs when they were ready to feed using their mouths. A special tooth helped them break the shell.

1. First, the mother dinosaur found a dry patch of ground, and she built a low mound, with a broad hollow area in the middle. She used her hands to do this.

2. Then she laid her eggs in the hollow, arranging them in careful circles, and burying the bottom part of each egg in the earth so they did not roll about.

3. She covered the eggs with some light soil and large rotting leaves. This formed a kind of compost on top that helped to keep the eggs warm.

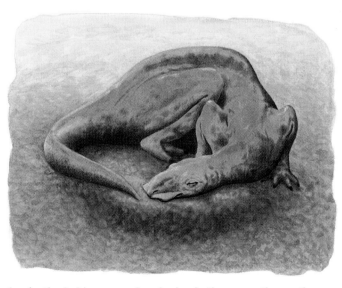

4. As the babies were developing in the eggs, the mother may have sat on the nest mound, partly to keep the eggs warm, and partly to protect them from egg-eating animals.

About Flying Reptiles?

PEOPLE THINK THAT dinosaurs could not fly. But, the most successful dinosaurs of all time could fly. What does this mean? Of course, the well-known dinosaurs could not fly, some of the small two-legged meat-eating dinosaurs evolved into birds some 150 million years ago. So, birds were once dinosaurs, which in a way means that birds are very successful living dinosaurs.

The most successful flyers in the age of the dinosaurs were the pterosaurs, 'winged reptiles', which lived for the same amount of time as the dinosaurs, from 225 million years ago, right to the great extinction 65 million years ago. The pterosaurs included the largest flying animals of all time, some as large as light aircraft.

Pterodactylus
This flying reptile was the size of a pigeon. A very successful fish-eater with jaws lined with tiny sharp teeth. *Pterodactylus* had no tail. Many species are known from many parts of the world.

Rhamphorhynchus
A dinosaur that lived at the same time as *Pterodactylus*, but was very different. It still had a long tail, and there was a curious '*rudder*' at the end of the tail, made from skin. Perhaps the tail was used in steering, but later pterosaurs had no tail.

Pteranodon
Pteranodon was for a long time the largest pterosaur known, and indeed the largest flying animal of all time, with a wingspan of 7 metres (22 feet). *Pteranodon* has long pointed jaws with no teeth, and a long counterbalance made from bone on the back of its head.

FLIGHT PATTERNS

Pterosaurs could fly, or they would not have had wings. But the very large ones must have had problems in flapping such huge wings. They probably flew by using currents of warm air that rise from the surface of the earth. This would allow them to soar.

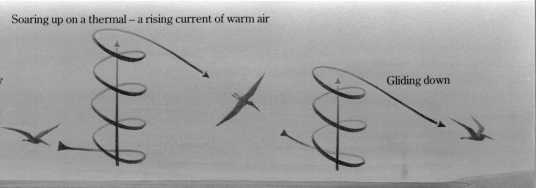

Soaring up on a thermal – a rising current of warm air

Gliding down

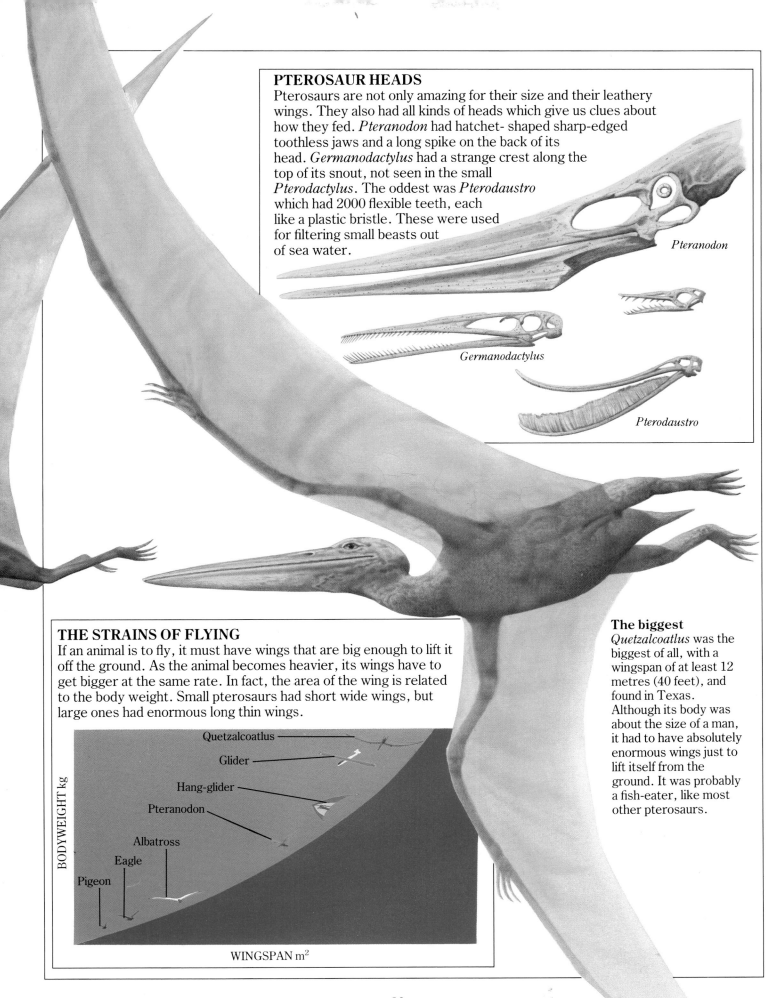

PTEROSAUR HEADS

Pterosaurs are not only amazing for their size and their leathery wings. They also had all kinds of heads which give us clues about how they fed. *Pteranodon* had hatchet- shaped sharp-edged toothless jaws and a long spike on the back of its head. *Germanodactylus* had a strange crest along the top of its snout, not seen in the small *Pterodactylus*. The oddest was *Pterodaustro* which had 2000 flexible teeth, each like a plastic bristle. These were used for filtering small beasts out of sea water.

Pteranodon

Germanodactylus

Pterodaustro

THE STRAINS OF FLYING

If an animal is to fly, it must have wings that are big enough to lift it off the ground. As the animal becomes heavier, its wings have to get bigger at the same rate. In fact, the area of the wing is related to the body weight. Small pterosaurs had short wide wings, but large ones had enormous long thin wings.

Quetzalcoatlus

Glider

Hang-glider

Pteranodon

Albatross

Eagle

Pigeon

BODYWEIGHT kg

WINGSPAN m²

The biggest

Quetzalcoatlus was the biggest of all, with a wingspan of at least 12 metres (40 feet), and found in Texas. Although its body was about the size of a man, it had to have absolutely enormous wings just to lift itself from the ground. It was probably a fish-eater, like most other pterosaurs.

Who Ruled the Sea?

DINOSAURS COULD SWIM, and often did. But the rulers of the seas were two other groups of extinct reptiles, the ichthyosaurs and the plesiosaurs. Both groups arose some time before the dinosaurs came on the scene, and the plesiosaurs at least lived right to the end of the age of the dinosaurs, 65 million years ago. But the ichthyosaurs seem to have died out about 90 million years ago. Both groups were hugely successful in the sea, and yet they arose from land-living animals.

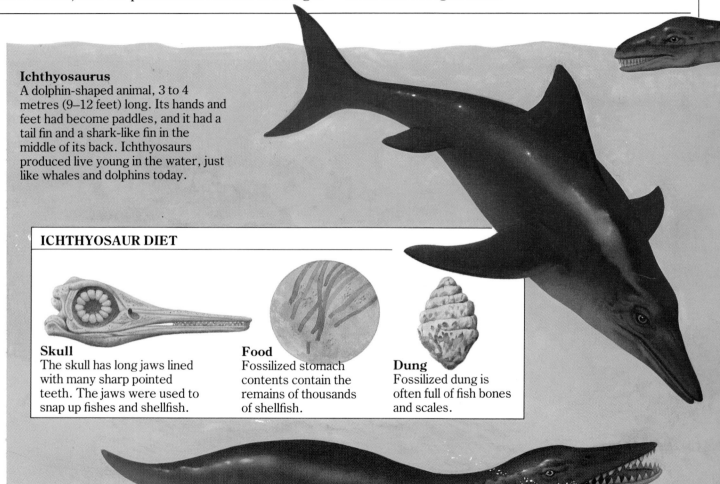

Ichthyosaurus
A dolphin-shaped animal, 3 to 4 metres (9–12 feet) long. Its hands and feet had become paddles, and it had a tail fin and a shark-like fin in the middle of its back. Ichthyosaurs produced live young in the water, just like whales and dolphins today.

ICHTHYOSAUR DIET

Skull
The skull has long jaws lined with many sharp pointed teeth. The jaws were used to snap up fishes and shellfish.

Food
Fossilized stomach contents contain the remains of thousands of shellfish.

Dung
Fossilized dung is often full of fish bones and scales.

Peloneustes
This is a special kind of plesiosaur called a pliosaur. It has a massive skull and a short neck, and probably fed on other smaller sea reptiles like ichthyosaurs.

Elasmosaurus
A remarkable long-necked plesiosaur. It has 40 or more bones in its neck, and it is likely that it could bend its neck around like a snake in order to catch fast-moving fishes.

EVOLUTION

The sea reptiles evolved from land-living animals, but the early stages in their evolution are not clear. Certainly the oldest ichthyosaurs and plesiosaurs did not have proper paddles, but still had the feet of land animals. There were many other sea reptiles, like shell-eating placodonts, giant mosasaurs, sea crocodiles, and even sea birds later on.

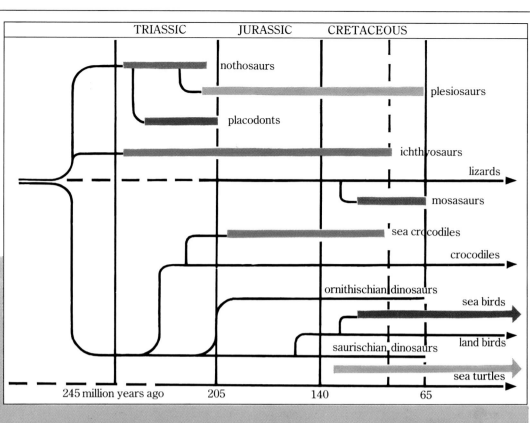

TRIASSIC JURASSIC CRETACEOUS

nothosaurs

plesiosaurs

placodonts

ichthyosaurs

lizards

mosasaurs

sea crocodiles

crocodiles

ornithischian dinosaurs

sea birds

land birds

saurischian dinosaurs

sea turtles

245 million years ago 205 140 65

TYPES OF SWIMMING

Some animals use their whole bodies for swimming, by throwing themselves into great curves; others just beat their tail from side to side or up and down, others 'fly' underwater, using their paddles, and some even row.

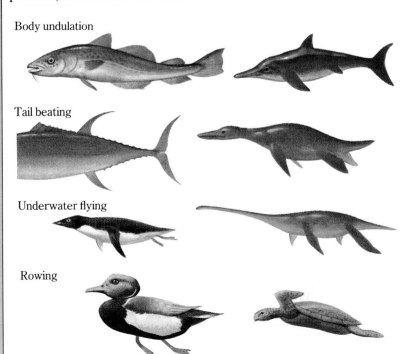

Body undulation

Tail beating

Underwater flying

Rowing

41

What Killed the Dinosaurs?

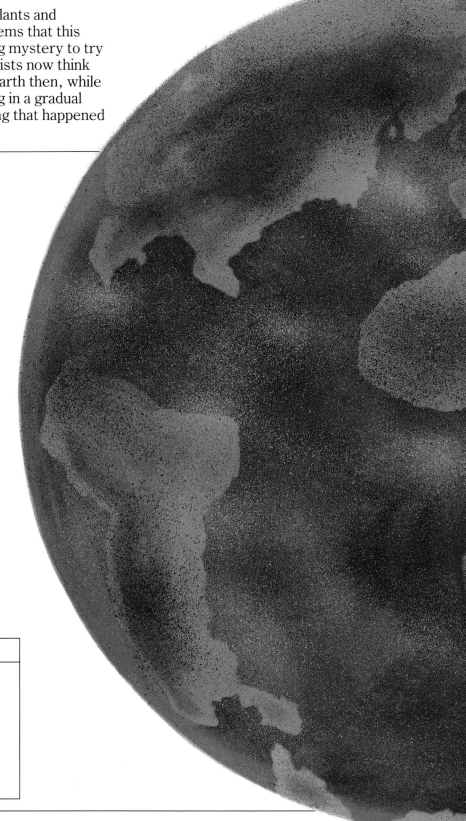

THE DINOSAURS, and many other kinds of plants and animals, died out 65 million years ago. It seems that this happened quite rapidly, and it is a fascinating mystery to try to find out just what happened. Many scientists now think that a giant meteorite, an *asteroid*, hit the Earth then, while others think that the climates were changing in a gradual way. No single theory can explain everything that happened so many years ago.

THE ASTEROID THEORY
The idea is that an asteroid, 10 kilometres (6 miles) across, hit the Earth and exploded. This would have sent a huge cloud of dust and rocks into the sky, which would have blacked out the Sun. Without sunlight, the air would freeze, and plants and animals would die. The dust then fell to Earth, and it has been found all over the world.

Dust layer
The 'dinosaur death dust layer' has been found in over 100 places around the world, in rocks that are exactly 65 million years old.

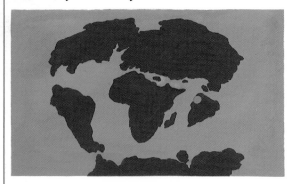

What lived and what died?

Died	Lived
Dinosaurs	Crocodiles
Pterosaurs	Birds
Plesiosaurs	Turtles
Mosasaurs	Lizards and snakes
Ammonites	Mammals
Belemnites	Fishes
Rudist bivalves	Insects
Foraminifera	Plants
	Most shellfish

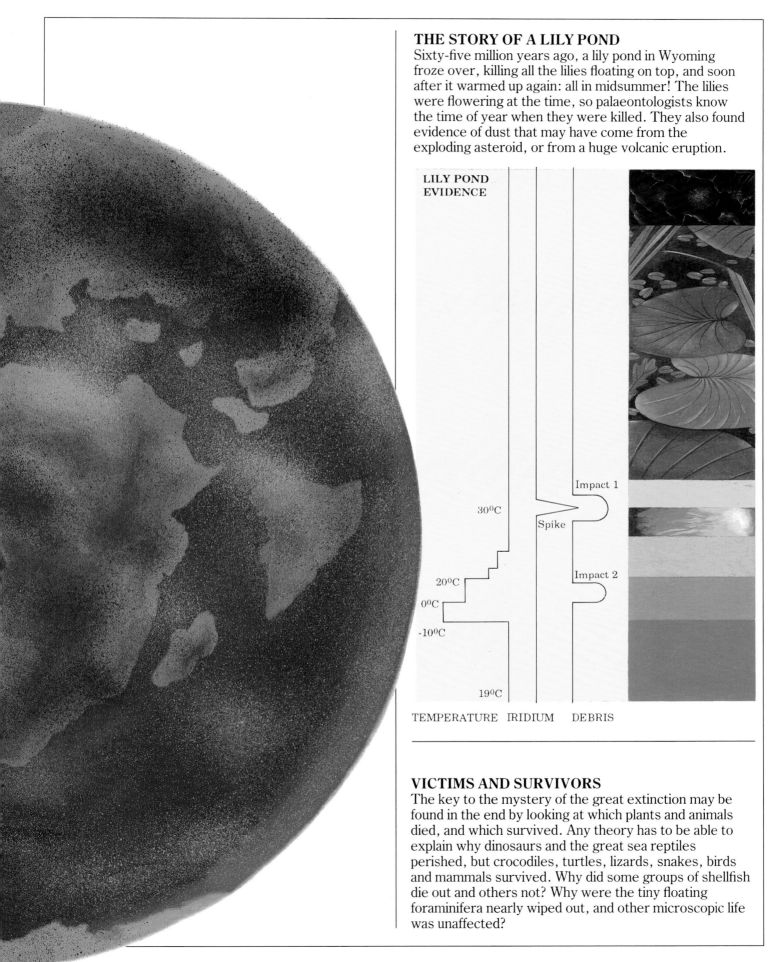

THE STORY OF A LILY POND
Sixty-five million years ago, a lily pond in Wyoming froze over, killing all the lilies floating on top, and soon after it warmed up again: all in midsummer! The lilies were flowering at the time, so palaeontologists know the time of year when they were killed. They also found evidence of dust that may have come from the exploding asteroid, or from a huge volcanic eruption.

LILY POND EVIDENCE

Impact 1

30°C

Spike

20°C

Impact 2

0°C

-10°C

19°C

TEMPERATURE IRIDIUM DEBRIS

VICTIMS AND SURVIVORS
The key to the mystery of the great extinction may be found in the end by looking at which plants and animals died, and which survived. Any theory has to be able to explain why dinosaurs and the great sea reptiles perished, but crocodiles, turtles, lizards, snakes, birds and mammals survived. Why did some groups of shellfish die out and others not? Why were the tiny floating foraminifera nearly wiped out, and other microscopic life was unaffected?

Glossary

Amphibian
A land animal, like a frog or salamander, that has to lay its eggs in water.

Ancestor
A plant or animal that gave rise to another, or to a whole group.

Asteroid
A large meteorite; a mass of rock that comes from space and may hit planets, like the Earth.

Blood stream
The flow of blood around the body, from the heart to the lungs and to the body.

Cold-blooded
Animals, like fishes and reptiles, that do not control their body temperatures as well as warm-blooded animals.

Evolution
The ways in which plants and animals have changed or adapted themselves from one form into another through time.

Gulley
A deep channel worn in sediment by heavy rain and rapid drainage.

Mummified
Dried out animal or human remains, where skin and other 'soft' parts may be preserved as well as the bone.

Nerves
Special cells in the body that send messages from the brain to the muscles or sense organs (eyes, ears, nose, tongue) and back again.

Porous
Containing holes or spaces.

Predator
A meat-eater; an animal that eats other animals, its prey.

Prospecting
Searching for dinosaurs, or other fossils, by hunting over the ground, looking for scraps and other clues.

Quarry
A hole in the ground which has been dug or blasted with explosives in order to take out rock or gravel for making buildings or roads.

Radioactive chemicals
Substances that change into others, and give off high-energy rays while doing so.

Rudder
A board fixed to the back of a boat, used in steering.

Snorkel
A breathing tube used by divers and other swimmers to allow them to breath under water.

Specimen
An example of a fossil or a rock.

Three-dimensional
Solid, not flat like a printed page, which is two-dimensional.

Tropical jungle
Large trees and plants that grow and live in hot damp parts of the world.

Warm-blooded
Animals, like birds and mammals, that keep their body temperatures constant.

Index